What Is the Nancy Drew?

by Dana Meachen Rau

illustrated by Dede Putra

Penguin Workshop

For the adventurous problem-solvers—DMR

For the Who HQ team—DP

PENGUIN WORKSHOP
An imprint of Penguin Random House LLC, New York

First published in the United States of America by Penguin Workshop,
an imprint of Penguin Random House LLC, New York, 2023

Visit us online at penguinrandomhouse.com.

Library of Congress Cataloging-in-Publication Data is available.

Printed in the United States of America

ISBN 9781524791797 (paperback)   10 9 8 7 6 5 4 3 2   WOR
ISBN 9781524791803 (library binding)   10 9 8 7 6 5 4 3 2 1 WOR

Contents

What Is the Story of Nancy Drew?

On a dark, rainy night, Nancy Drew sneaked out after bedtime to investigate an old stone house next door. Nancy was no stranger to danger. She was brave and followed her instincts. When she investigated a mystery, she never gave up until the case was solved.

As she explored inside the old house, she realized she was not alone. A maid was searching the house, certain that she had heard a noise. Nancy rushed to hide. She barely escaped getting caught. But she found herself locked in a room with no way out. "Now I am in a mess!" she said.

In the back of the closet, she felt a tiny knob and gave it a twist. *Click!* With a push, the wall opened, and Nancy suddenly fell down a flight of stairs, into the dark. Nancy was shaken. She turned on her flashlight and saw a narrow passageway. She didn't know where it led, but it was her only escape.

Nancy Drew isn't a real person. This curious and independent teenage detective is a character in a series of books written by Carolyn Keene. When the first books in the Nancy Drew Mystery Stories series were published in 1930, girls and young women were not encouraged to be adventurous. But Nancy didn't follow those rules.

No one told her she couldn't do something just because she was a girl. In fact, she often did things better than the men in her stories! Nancy's character was popular, friendly, and kind. She was talented, smart, and thoughtful. She helped people in need and fought for fairness. Nancy had it all!

Readers have been enjoying Nancy Drew mysteries for more than ninety years. Over

that time, Nancy has been chased, kidnapped, poisoned, and locked in closets. She has ridden horses, flown airplanes, explored haunted houses, and been attacked by a robot. Most readers would never have the kind of life Nancy has! But this famous detective's luck and skill have inspired readers around the world to be curious, daring, and fearless as they face any of life's challenges.

CHAPTER 1
Big-City Book Business

The many stories about the character Nancy Drew have made her one of the most popular girl detectives of all time. But where did her own story begin? The key to this mystery starts in New Jersey.

Edward Stratemeyer was born in Elizabeth, New Jersey, in 1862. As a child, he loved to read adventure stories. He filled his shelves with books about poor boys who became wealthy heroes through hard work and bravery. He also read books about

Edward Stratemeyer

boys who traveled the world, fought in wars, explored the American West, and sailed the seas. Besides reading, Edward also liked to write his own adventure stories and even published a newspaper as a teenager.

Edward's father didn't think writing would be a good job for his son. So Edward worked as a clerk in his brother's shop. He still wrote, though. In the late 1800s, many children read stories in story papers and magazines that came out weekly and monthly. Hoping they would be published, Edward sent them his stories. When he was in his twenties, he sold a story called "Victor Horton's Idea" to *Golden Days* magazine and made seventy-five dollars. It was published in 1889, and he decided writing would be his career.

Edward married Magdalene (called Lenna) and they soon had two daughters, Harriet and Edna. He tried out his own story ideas on the girls. Each night, they got just a bit of a story. They would have to wait until the next night to find out what

happened next. Edward wrote a series called the Rover Boys, which became a huge success. His Bobbsey Twins series was also popular. Kids loved Edward's books and couldn't wait for more. This was not a problem for Edward. He had plenty of ideas.

Edward had been working for Street & Smith, a children's book and magazine publisher. In 1905, he decided to start his own company, called the Stratemeyer Syndicate, first working from home and then from offices in New York City. (*Syndicate* is another word for "group.") He came up with the ideas, created the characters, and outlined stories for the book series. Then he hired authors, called ghostwriters, to write the books.

Stratemeyer Syndicate
Books for Boys and Girls

He created pen names (made-up author names) for each series so that all the books in the series would seem like they were written by one person when, really, they were written by many. That way, he could create books in different series in much less time. A publisher would then print and sell the books.

The Stratemeyer Syndicate's series sold by the millions! In 1926, the Syndicate had more than thirty book series in publication. In a survey that same year, 98 percent of kids listed a book by the Stratemeyer Syndicate as their favorite. Edward became rich!

Edward never stopped thinking of new ideas. Detective stories were becoming more popular with adults. So he thought young readers might like them, too. In 1927, Edward started the Hardy Boys series. In it, brothers Frank and Joe Hardy face danger as they solve crimes. The Hardy Boys was a big hit with readers. Edward

thought the Syndicate should have a similar series featuring a strong female character. He sent his idea to his publisher, describing his girl detective as "bright, clever, resourceful, and full of energy." He thought she should be named Stella Strong. The publishers loved the idea but not the name. From a list of his other name ideas, they chose Nan Drew—which later became Nancy.

Now Edward needed to find a ghostwriter. He had just the right person—a young writer from Iowa named Mildred Augustine.

Mildred Augustine

Ghostwriters

A ghostwriter is someone who writes a book but whose name does not appear as the author. The ghostwriter is paid to write for someone else.

Imagine a famous person has an amazing story to tell but doesn't have the time or skills to write it. They could hire a ghostwriter. The famous person is  officially credited as the author, even though the ghostwriter did most or all of the writing.

They are called "ghostwriters" because they remain (mostly) invisible and unknown.

CHAPTER 2
Small-Town Writer

As the Stratemeyer Syndicate grew in New York City, Mildred Augustine was growing up far away, in a small town in Iowa. Mildred was born on July 10, 1905. She spent hours playing adventurous games and making up stories with her paper dolls. Like Edward Stratemeyer, Mildred loved to read and write, too.

When she was thirteen, she entered her story "The Courtesy" in a contest run by the popular children's magazine *St. Nicholas*. It was published in the June 1919 issue, announcing she had won the Silver Badge award.

Mildred left her small town for college at the State University of Iowa in 1922. She took classes in the new journalism program that trained students to become writers. She got plenty of practice working for the college newspaper. She also played sports, including soccer, basketball, and swimming. And she was really good at playing the xylophone! After graduation in June 1925, she went to work for the *Clinton Herald* newspaper.

Mildred still wanted to write stories for children. In 1926, she answered a magazine advertisement from the Stratemeyer Syndicate that said it was looking for authors. Mildred met with Edward Stratemeyer in New York City. Soon after, he hired her. While writing books for

Stratemeyer, Mildred went back to school to get another college degree in journalism. She also married Asa Wirt and moved to Cleveland, Ohio. Through it all, she kept in touch with Edward.

In 1929, when Edward needed a ghostwriter for his new girl detective series, he thought of twenty-four-year-old Mildred Augustine Wirt. He asked if she would be interested in writing the first three books in the Nancy Drew Mystery Stories series for $125 each. She said yes. So he sent her his three-and-a-half-page outline for the first book—*The Secret of the Old Clock*.

Mildred wrote a story full of action and suspense, just like Edward wanted. She then wrote the next two books in the series: *The Hidden Staircase* and *The Bungalow Mystery*.

Following Edward's ideas, Mildred helped create a unique girl with an unbelievable talent for solving mysteries. The character Nancy Drew is sixteen years old and lives in the town of River Heights. Her father, Carson Drew, is a lawyer. Her mother died when she was little, and so Nancy is in charge of running the household. She does have

some help from the family's maid, an older woman named Hannah Gruen. The Drews have plenty of money, and Nancy seems to have few worries. Her days are filled with shopping, visiting friends, going to parties, and running errands for her father in her very own car: a blue convertible, known as a roadster.

Nancy spends most of her time following clues to solve mysteries. Her curiosity, intelligence, and hard work lead her on adventure after adventure. Nancy's life is nonstop action. Car

chases! Spy missions! Underground explorations! Nancy stands up to criminals and always saves the day. She's so good that the police and her father often come to *her* for advice.

History of Mystery!

As more people moved into cities in the nineteenth century, and crime rates went up, police departments needed to hire more crime-solving detectives. Authors began to introduce detectives as characters in their stories, too.

Edgar Allan Poe

The first detective story was written by the American author Edgar Allan Poe in 1841. In "The Murders in the Rue Morgue," his detective, C. Auguste Dupin, investigates a murder, gathers clues, and uncovers who—or what—is to blame for a crime. Later in the century, Sir Arthur Conan Doyle created one of the most famous detectives:

Sherlock Holmes. Holmes was able to solve his cases by close observation, logical reasoning, and scientific knowledge.

Detective stories and novels became even more popular in the early part of the 1900s. In the 1920s, British author Agatha Christie started writing detective mysteries. Since then, her books, about Hercule Poirot and Miss Jane Marple, have sold more than one hundred million copies, and she has become one of the most famous mystery authors of all time.

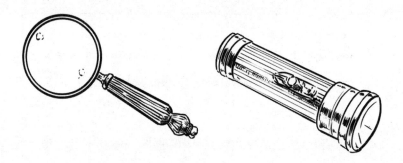

The first three Nancy Drew Mystery Stories were released in April 1930 and used the pen name Carolyn Keene as the author. Before long, readers couldn't get enough of this friendly, clever, and fearless girl detective.

CHAPTER 3
Nancy on the Case

The Secret of the Old Clock, the first book in the Nancy Drew Mystery Stories series, begins with a conversation between Nancy and her father, Carson Drew. They are discussing a man they both knew, wealthy Josiah Crowley.

When Josiah had grown old, he moved himself and all of his belongings in with his relatives,  the Tophams. When the story begins, Josiah has just died. His will—the legal document that indicates who will inherit his money and property— states that his fortune will go to the Topham family. Nancy doesn't think this is fair. She suspects that the Tophams only took care of Josiah so that they could have control of his money, and that they had persuaded him to leave it all to them. Later, while buying a dress at a department store, Nancy even overhears the Topham daughters, Ada and Isabel, plotting how they are going to spend their new fortune.

A few days later, while running errands, Nancy gets caught in a horrible storm. She parks her shiny blue roadster in a barn for shelter.

Here, she meets the Horner sisters, young women who live alone because their parents have died. They are poor yet warm and welcoming. Nancy finds out that Josiah Crowley was like an uncle to them. He had told them he would leave them money in his will. Nancy feels sure there could be a second will that might include the Horners. She is determined to find it. "I'm not going to give up!" Nancy says.

Nancy visits other relatives and friends of Josiah Crowley. They all tell Nancy that Josiah had promised to leave them money in his will. An elderly friend of Josiah, Abigail Rowen, provides Nancy with clues. When Abigail's clock chimes, she remembers that Josiah had told her about a notebook that held some important information. Somehow, Josiah's own clock and the notebook were connected. Nancy decides she must find Josiah's clock.

She visits the Tophams' house, hoping to find

it. But Nancy is disappointed to see that their clock doesn't look like the one Abigail had described. In front of the family, Nancy pretends to admire it. And through her clever questions, she finds out  that Josiah's clock is at the Tophams' cottage on Moon Lake. She takes her roadster on the long trip. At the cottage, the doors are open, the house is a mess, and the furniture is missing. She's arrived in the middle of a robbery!

Nancy finds a safe place to hide in a closet. But the dust makes her sneeze, and the thieves discover her. She struggles to get away, but they lock the closet door and leave her there. When she breaks out, Nancy goes to the police, and they hurry to chase after the thieves. Nancy leads the way in her roadster until they have to split up at a fork in the road. She's the one who finds the burglars' van parked in a stable near an old inn. She sneaks into it, finds the clock, and hides until the men leave. She runs back to her own car. Before she races to the police, she excitedly unscrews the clock's

face. It is there that she discovers Josiah Crowley's tiny blue notebook!

After the police catch the thieves, Nancy reads the notebook safely back at her home. It reveals that Josiah did indeed hide a second will in a safe-deposit box at the bank. The story ends with everyone gathered at the Drew house. Mr. Drew reads the will, and it is filled with good news. Josiah has left money to his friends and relatives. He did not leave anything to the Topham family. The Horner sisters want to reward Nancy. But Nancy won't accept money. She asks for the clock instead. "I'll always prize this clock as a trophy of my first venture as a detective," she says.

Two more Nancy Drew Mystery Stories came out at the same time as *The Secret of the Old Clock*: *The Hidden Staircase* and *The Bungalow Mystery*. In *The Hidden Staircase*, Nancy investigates a haunted house. The elderly Turnbull sisters have been hearing voices and seeing shadows. And even worse— expensive items have gone missing! Nancy doesn't

believe in ghosts. She thinks there must be an explanation. She discovers a hidden staircase and tunnel between the Turnbull house and the next, where a nasty man has been sneaking back and forth. Nancy, as always, is fearless and solves the case. The Turnbull sisters give her a silver urn— a tall metal vase—as a reward for her help.

In the first scene of *The Bungalow Mystery*, Nancy and her friend Helen are stranded in a boat during a dangerous storm on Moon Lake. Nancy saves Helen from drowning and then is saved herself by a girl named Laura. Nancy repays the favor by helping Laura solve a mystery around her new guardian, who seems to want Laura's money. Throughout this story, Nancy hides in bushes, trespasses on private property, and is tied with ropes in a basement dungeon. Even through car chases and explosions, Nancy uses her luck, skill, and bravery to get back Laura's fortune. Laura gives Nancy precious jewels to remember another mystery solved!

"I seem to have a way of getting into the thick of things," Nancy says. She always seems to have a way of getting herself out, too! With her help, the good guys always win, and the criminals are always caught. Nancy is the hero of every story.

CHAPTER 4
An Adventurous Girl in Charge!

During the Great Depression, from 1929 to 1939, many people lost their jobs and didn't have much money to spend. But still, thousands of copies of the first Nancy Drew Mystery Stories were sold. Edward Stratemeyer was a smart businessperson. He had insisted that the books only cost fifty cents so that children could still afford them, even as the country struggled through such a difficult time. Readers loved the stories about Nancy—a character who didn't seem affected by the troubles of the Depression. She was a smart girl who could solve problems if she worked hard enough. And that was something readers wanted to believe about themselves, too.

The books had many fans who loved the way they were written. The stories featured mysterious settings, like abandoned cottages, haunted houses, and dusty, dark attics. Nancy always seemed swept up in impossible situations.

She was stalked by wild animals, lost in dark tunnels, and locked in rooms with no escape. Each book followed the same formula: twenty-five action-packed chapters, each with a cliff-hanger ending. That meant that each chapter ended in suspense. Kids were eager to keep reading to find out what happened in the very next chapter. After they finished one book, they would rush to buy the next.

Readers liked that the Nancy Drew Mystery Stories, and all of Stratemeyer's series, weren't like other children's books at the time. Most books for kids up to the early 1900s were filled with lessons about how to be good. The adults in the stories always knew best. But in Nancy's mysteries, the adults never seemed to tell her what to do. Nancy's father, and many of the other adults in River Heights, often asked for her help. Readers felt powerful reading about a teenage character who was in charge.

Most importantly, Nancy was a new type of role model for girls. Female characters in stories at this time were often helpless and needed to be rescued. They let others make decisions for them. That was true for many young women at the time, too.

Leading up to the 1930s, boys and girls had very defined roles. Boys were trained to be in charge when they grew up, to run businesses, and to make the money to support their families. Parents told boys that they could become anything they wanted to be. Girls, on the other hand, were trained to take care of the home. While boys explored the outdoors and played adventure games, girls played "house" by dressing dolls and holding tea parties. Their job was to become wives and mothers. They were not expected to have careers of their own. In fact, it wasn't until 1920, just ten years before the first Nancy Drew books were published, that women even had the right to vote.

Nancy was different. She showed girls and young women that it was okay to be in charge.

Nancy had the same skills as many boys. She could change tires on her car, play sports, solve problems, and take risks. She was always confident, even when she was afraid. But at the same time, she still acted like most people expected girls to behave at that time: She was kind and friendly. She always wore fashionable

clothes. She could garden, draw, and bake. It seemed as if she could do anything! Girls liked Nancy because at the end of each story, people thanked her, celebrated her, and offered her rewards for saving the day.

While young readers loved the Nancy Drew Mystery Stories, some adults didn't. Librarians didn't think adventure and detective series were a good influence on younger readers. They still wanted children to read stories filled with lessons that taught manners and good behavior. But the librarians' complaints actually helped the books sell. If adults didn't like them, then kids wanted to read them even more!

Sadly, Edward Stratemeyer wasn't able to see the success of his Nancy Drew series. Only twelve days after the first three Nancy books were published, Edward died. He was sixty-seven years old. In his will, Edward left the company to his family, thinking that they would sell it. But since the country was struggling because of the Depression, no one could afford to buy it. Edward's wife, Lenna, was not healthy enough to run it herself. But his two daughters—

Harriet Stratemeyer Adams, age thirty-seven, and Edna Stratemeyer, age thirty-four—could. They took over running the Stratemeyer Syndicate.

Nancy Drew's future was now in their hands.

Behind the Wheel

In the early 1930s, less than 20 percent of Americans owned cars. And those who did were mostly men. But from the very first book in the Nancy Drew Mystery Stories series, Nancy drove her own car. Nancy's father had given it to her as a gift for her sixteenth birthday. Not only is she an excellent driver, but she can even change her own flat tire.

Nancy's car became a symbol of independence. Behind the wheel, she could go wherever she needed or wanted to. She had the freedom to chase after clues, or criminals, and save the day. She could travel around her small town on her own or go beyond its borders for new adventures. It was a freedom that few people had.

Nancy's car has changed over the years. In early stories, her car is a shiny blue 1930s two-seat

Then

roadster. Its color changed a few times, to maroon, black, and green. In later Nancy Drew books, it is called a coupe and also a convertible. In the 1980s, it is described as a red car. In recent books, Nancy does her part to help the environment by driving a blue hybrid.

Now

CHAPTER 5
More Friends and Adventures for Nancy

Harriet and Edna decided to move the Stratemeyer Syndicate from New York City to East Orange, New Jersey, closer to their own homes. They were now in charge of all the jobs their father had done—hiring writers, sending out outlines, and editing series. Edna left the company after about ten years, but Harriet kept it going. Harriet had always wanted a career, but she had followed the path most women did at the time—getting married and raising a family. Now she was able to run a business. And she was very good at it!

Harriet continued to hire Mildred Augustine Wirt to write the Nancy Drew Mystery Stories as Carolyn Keene. Harriet had lots of ideas for Nancy's next adventures. The outlines she sent to Mildred were even more detailed than her father's had been.

Harriet and Mildred sometimes disagreed about which parts of Nancy's character were most important. Harriet rewrote parts of Mildred's work. She made sure that Mildred's bold Nancy was still soft and kindhearted. For a few books, Mildred took a break from writing.

During that time, Walter Karig wrote as Carolyn Keene for three stories. But soon, Mildred was back.

Walter Karig

New characters began appearing in the books. In the fifth book in the series, *The Secret at Shadow Ranch*, readers meet cousins Bess and George for the first time. Nancy joins these friends on a summer vacation to their uncle's ranch in Arizona.

Bess Marvin is an attractive girl with proper manners. She always says and does the right thing. But she's also worried and easily afraid. George Fayne is the opposite. Instead of having long hair like Bess, George's is cut short, like

a boy's. She is skinny, tough, and confident. Together, Bess, George, and Nancy ride horses, fight off wild animals, hide in caves, and rescue a kidnapped little girl.

Ned Nickerson appears for the first time in

the seventh book, *The Clue in the Diary*. While Nancy investigates a burning house, she catches a boy stealing her car! She realizes that he was just kindly moving it out of the way of the fire. Ned is a college student who plays football.

Over time in the series, he becomes her boyfriend. But unlike most girls her age, Nancy isn't looking for romance. Ned is more of a friend who sometimes helps her with cases.

Nancy gets a pet in the fourteenth book of the series, *The Whispering Statue*. While at a park with

Bess and George, Nancy spots a dog snatching someone's purse. Nancy helps get the purse back and finds clues inside to her next mystery. When  the dog follows her, she ends up bringing him home and naming him Togo. The dog isn't in every Nancy story, but Togo does pop in and out over the history of the series.

The number of Nancy fans grew throughout the 1930s, as Nancy got herself into and out of more sticky situations. Nancy faces car crashes, train accidents, fires, and ghosts. She recovers stolen jewels and large fortunes, and helps orphans. She's tied up, kidnapped, and framed for crimes. Nancy Drew had an exciting—and dangerous—decade!

Who Drew Nancy Drew?

Russell H. Tandy (1891–1963) illustrated the Nancy Drew Mystery Stories covers throughout the 1930s and 1940s. Tandy was born in Brooklyn, New York. He went to art school in New York City. After he graduated, he went on to draw pictures for sewing patterns and clothing catalogs. So he was a good choice to draw the stylish and fashionable Nancy Drew.

Tandy read through each story to decide which scene was best to illustrate for the cover. He drew Nancy as a well-dressed teenager who wore hats, suits, and heels. He also gave her golden blond curls and bright blue eyes. Russell H. Tandy illustrated more than twenty covers for the Nancy Drew Mystery Stories.

Bryan Foy

In the 1930s, with the success of the books at an all-time high, Nancy Drew also began appearing on movie screens. Bryan Foy headed the part of Warner Brothers studio that produced B movies. B movies were the second movie of a double feature. They were usually shorter, part of a series, and cost less money to make than the main movie.

Foy got the idea to make Nancy movies from his own daughter: She had asked him for a set of Nancy Drew books for Christmas. By then, there were fourteen books in the series. But Foy couldn't find them anywhere. The books were sold out! He figured if readers loved Nancy's character in the books, they would probably come to see her in the movies as well.

The studio chose Bonita Granville, a fifteen-year-old actress with blond, curly hair, to play Nancy, and the actor Frankie Thomas to play Ned Nickerson, who was called Ted in the films.

Bonita Granville

Four black-and-white Nancy Drew movies came out between November 1938 and September 1939.

The first movie, *Nancy Drew: Detective*, is loosely based on the story of the tenth book, *The Password to Larkspur Lane*. A wealthy woman named Miss Eldridge is planning on donating money to Nancy's school. But she suddenly leaves town. Nancy soon discovers that Miss Eldridge has been kidnapped! Unlike in the books, the adults in the movie don't seem to respect Nancy. Her father warns her to stop her investigation because it's too dangerous. The police tell her that she should go home and play with her dolls. While the movie is filled with adventure and suspense, it is a comedy. The characters are silly and get themselves into ridiculous situations.

But in some ways, the movie does capture the true spirit of Nancy. She drives her own car, flies in an airplane, hides in a car trunk, sneaks into a house, and of course, solves the mystery!

CHAPTER 6
Changing with the Times

Ghostwriter Mildred Augustine Wirt had a very busy schedule, writing a new Nancy Drew book almost every year through the 1940s and into the 1950s. Her last was *The Clue of the Velvet Mask* in 1953. In all, she had written twenty-three books for the Nancy Drew Mystery Stories series. But Mildred wasn't the only author writing under the name Carolyn Keene. A few other authors contributed as well, including Harriet Stratemeyer. In fact, Harriet took over writing the Nancy books in the mid-1950s. The character of Nancy Drew

was very special to her. Harriet liked to think of Nancy as her own daughter.

During her adventures, Nancy saved family fortunes, tracked down thieves, and rescued people from kidnappers. She explored haunted boats, mansions, and bridges. She rode in planes, ships, trains, and of course, her trusty roadster. She

traveled to New Orleans, Virginia, Pennsylvania, Canada, and Boston. She met scientists, inventors, actors, ballet dancers, circus performers, treasure hunters, and musicians. She even found a map to buried treasure. Bess, George, and Ned came along on many of her cases.

In the 1940s, the United States was involved in World War II, and many men in the United States left their homes to fight in the war. Some women who stayed at home took jobs that were traditionally held by men.

Women working during World War II

They liked Nancy's independent spirit and encouraged their daughters to read the series. In the 1950s, after the war had ended, some women returned to their roles as homemakers. Nancy still appealed to so many readers because she was successful at everything she tried. In one chapter, she might make a daring escape from danger, and in the next, she baked a cake!

But Harriet felt that Nancy was starting to feel a bit old-fashioned. Readers of the late 1950s were very different from readers twenty years earlier. And kids weren't reading as much as they once had because television was taking over as a major source of entertainment. So in 1959, Harriet decided to make major changes to the Nancy Drew Mystery Stories series.

Harriet and her team worked to revise the old stories, starting with the first one, *The Secret of the Old Clock*. The books, which had

always been twenty-five chapters long, were shortened to twenty. Harriet felt this faster pace would keep readers' attention. Some books just had small changes. For example, in the new version of *The Secret of the Old Clock*,

Harriet and the revised version of *The Secret of the Old Clock*

the Horner sisters are now called the Hoovers, and there is no mention of a shoot-out with the robbers before they are arrested. Harriet also added in a few new characters—a little girl named Judy and a singing teacher named Signor Mascagni.

Some of the stories were completely rewritten.

In *The Secret at Shadow Ranch*, published in 1931, Nancy handles a gun, shoots a lynx, and rescues a kidnapped girl. In the revised book, *The Secret of Shadow Ranch*, published in 1965, the ranch is haunted by a ghost horse, and Nancy uncovers a romance from the past and a hidden treasure.

Harriet also made changes to Nancy's character. Even though Harriet was a strong woman herself, she thought that the Nancy in the old books was sometimes too bold. In the revisions, Nancy doesn't talk back to adults or break the law. She is always positive. She doesn't get angry or afraid.

But she still has her trusty friends Bess, George, and Ned by her side.

During the revision process, Harriet made an effort to be sure the details fit the current times. Nancy's age went from sixteen to eighteen because in some states, the driving age was eighteen. Nancy also got a new dark-blue convertible. Other details about the technology of the times changed, too. Nancy no longer sent telegrams or put food in an icebox. Instead she made phone calls and used a refrigerator!

The books also needed to be revised to be more respectful to all groups of people. Some parents and teachers had complained that the books treated people of color, immigrants, and certain religious groups unfairly. The revisions tried to remove some of the series' harmful stereotypes.

Nancy's look also changed. Harriet hired a new illustrator for the covers in 1953. Rudy Nappi had already designed many covers for detective magazines and other Stratemeyer Syndicate books. Now he worked to update the Nancy Drew covers. The new Nancy's hair was more red than blond. Instead of solving her cases in full suits, hats, and heels, she wore more current fashions—even jeans. Nappi illustrated the Nancy books into the late 1970s.

In 1962, the publishers started to produce the books with a bright yellow spine. That way, they were easy to spot and more desirable to collect. Many readers had full sets of Nancy's yellow-spined books on their bookshelves. Nancy Drew books had been published in many other countries. By the late 1960s, readers all over the world collected them. Sometimes Nancy's name changed. In Finland, she was Paula Drew. In Sweden, she was Kitty Drew. In Germany, her new name was Susanne Langen, and in France, readers knew her as Alice Roy.

Fan Mail

The Stratemeyer Syndicate received lots of fan mail from readers who didn't realize the pen names on the books weren't real people. Harriet  and Edna sometimes wrote back to the eager fans on behalf of the authors, as if they were real. They worked hard to protect the secret that the series were written by ghostwriters.

Fans wrote to tell Carolyn Keene how much they liked her stories and asked her to write more. Some even wrote with story suggestions and hopes for more romance between Nancy and Ned. A magazine even tried to contact Ms. Keene to write a story for them! In the 1960s, the Syndicate had an office assistant who worked almost full-time answering fan mail for their various authors.

CHAPTER 7
Beyond the Books

Harriet continued to take on the role of author, as Carolyn Keene, adding exciting new settings to the Nancy Drew Mystery Stories series. During the 1960s and 1970s, Nancy visited Hong Kong in *The Mystery of the Fire Dragon* to investigate a mysterious dragon symbol. She visits her great-grandmother in Scotland and tracks down her family history in *The Clue of the Whistling Bagpipes*. In Peru, she cracks a code that leads to treasure in *The Clue in the Crossword Cipher*. She goes on an African safari in *The Spider Sapphire Mystery*. In Istanbul, she discovers a message in a Turkish rug in *The Mysterious Mannequin*.

The books didn't just introduce readers to new locations; they also showed off new technologies.

In *The Crooked Banister*, Nancy encounters a robot guarding a strange house. When she gets too close, the robot squeezes her so hard that she passes out! Nancy discovers that if she inserts the right program, the robot can actually help her solve a case. In *Mystery of the Glowing Eye*, Nancy searches for Ned. He's been kidnapped because he's been developing a high-powered laser light in his college laboratory, and the bad guys want to get their hands on it.

The character of Nancy Drew also moved beyond her famous series of books. She showed up in coloring books, on puzzles, as paper dolls, and on the sides of lunch boxes. In 1957, Parker Brothers released the Nancy Drew Mystery Game. Families and friends could gather around a game board covered with important spots from Nancy's history, such as the Haunted Bridge, the Old Attic, and Blackwood Hall. The object of the game was to find Nancy's location. It came with a stack of character mystery cards and tiny colored metal cars to "drive" around the board.

In 1967, the Madame Alexander Doll Company created a Nancy Drew doll. Doll collectors enjoyed this tiny version of Nancy. She wore a two-piece suit, boots, and a scarf around her neck. The doll came with sunglasses, a red purse, and a camera, everything Nancy needed for her mystery adventures.

Next, Nancy made her way into the kitchen with *The Nancy Drew Cookbook* in 1973. The recipes all had names connected to book titles in the series, such as Crumbling Wall Coffee Cake (from *The Clue in the Crumbling Wall*), Blackwood Hall Muffins (from *The Ghost of Blackwood Hall*), Brass-Bound Trunk Candy (from *The Mystery of the Brass-Bound Trunk*), and Larkspur Lane Sandwiches (from *The Password to Larkspur Lane*). The cookbook encouraged readers to be adventurers in the kitchen by trying out new recipes.

In January 1977, kids were finally able to watch Nancy Drew on television. The ABC network aired a show called *The Nancy Drew Mysteries*. It alternated weeks with another new show—*The Hardy Boys Mysteries*. Twenty-four-year-old Pamela Sue Martin starred as Nancy, who worked as a private investigator for her lawyer father. The hour-long show was filled with action, just like the books. Instead of cliff-hanger moments at the end of each chapter, during each commercial break viewers would be left wondering what would happen next.

The two shows were combined into *The Hardy Boys/Nancy Drew Mysteries* the next year, and then the Hardy Boys show continued without Nancy for another year.

In the 1970s, librarians who had not yet done so were finally convinced that the Nancy Drew Mystery Stories were worthy enough to be added to library collections. With television becoming so popular, they agreed that series books were a good way to keep kids excited about reading.

CHAPTER 8
So Many New Nancys!

The year 1980 was huge for Nancy Drew. She celebrated her fiftieth anniversary! In her honor, the publisher held a party at the Harkness House—a fancy mansion on Fifth Avenue in New York City.

Ruth Bader Ginsburg with a blue roadster at the Nancy Drew fiftieth anniversary party, 1980

The five-hundred-person guest list included famous actors, singers, writers, and journalists. Even judge Ruth Bader Ginsburg, a Nancy Drew fan who later became a Supreme Court justice, attended the event. A blue roadster was parked out front. Guests were each given a mini flashlight that they used while walking through a spooky cave.

Actors dressed as characters greeted guests all evening throughout the four floors of the mansion. There was Ned, Bess, George, police officers, criminals, and two Nancys— one from the 1930s and one from the 1980s. Guests had a mystery to solve, too. Every hour, a new clue was announced. By the end of the evening, it was revealed that the butler had stolen a band member's emerald pin.

The same year Nancy turned fifty, fans wondered about another big mystery: Who *was* Carolyn Keene? Most readers had always

Guests pose with 1930s Nancy Drew character at the
Nancy Drew fiftieth anniversary party, 1980

thought Keene was a real person. She received
tons of fan letters at the Stratemeyer Syndicate.
In 1980, Nancy became part of a real court case.

Publishers were deciding who had the rights to publish the Nancy Drew stories. During the trial, the identity of Carolyn Keene came up. Harriet Stratemeyer Adams claimed that she had written all the books since 1930. But Mildred (now Mildred Wirt Benson since she had remarried) was then called in as a witness. She proved that she had been the earliest author of the series. By the end of the trial, the world knew that Mildred, now seventy-five years old, and Harriet, eighty-seven, should share credit for creating and developing the much-loved character.

After Nancy Drew's fiftieth anniversary, more books were published than ever before. The original Nancy Drew Mystery Stories series continued, with Harriet writing the next few titles. When she died in 1982, the series continued with other ghostwriters until 2003, with *Werewolf in a Winter Wonderland*. Nancy had come a long way from Book 1 to Book 175.

Mildred Wirt Benson

Mildred Augustine Wirt Benson (1905–2002)

Mildred, the original Carolyn Keene, was born in Ladora, Iowa. She lived through most of the twentieth century, watching the role of women change over the course of her lifetime. "I just naturally thought that girls could do the things boys did," Mildred once said.

Like Nancy, Mildred seemed able to do it all. She

was the first woman to graduate from the school of journalism at the University of Iowa and the first person to get a master's in journalism from there. She married twice and had one child. She wrote more than 130 children's books, some for the Stratemeyer Syndicate and many under her own name as well. She worked as a journalist at a time when most reporters were men. She liked adventure, and at age fifty-nine she got her pilot's license. She became fascinated with archaeology and explored sites in Central America. In her eighties, she even applied to be an astronaut and work as a journalist in space.

Mildred wrote a column for the *Toledo Blade* newspaper until she died in 2002 at the age of ninety-six. She donated her typewriter, on which she wrote some of the Nancy Drew mysteries, to the National Museum of American History in Washington, DC.

In this final story, Nancy enjoys the River Heights Winter Carnival and ends up investigating wolves that are missing from a nature preserve. Nancy bravely encounters avalanches, fires, and car accidents. But unlike the Nancy of earlier books, this Nancy drinks lattes, eats pizza, listens to CDs

in her car, and talks on her cell phone. Bess and George are still her best friends, Ned is still her boyfriend, and Hannah Gruen still welcomes her home.

Meanwhile, starting in 1986, another Nancy series tried to attract a slightly older audience.

(The original series was for readers ages eight to eleven.) This new series, the Nancy Drew Files, for readers eleven to fourteen, introduced a more modern Nancy. She still lived in River Heights and hung around with Bess, George, and Ned. But her cases were more violent and dangerous. In the first book, *Secrets Can Kill*, Nancy goes undercover and solves a mystery of nighttime break-ins at the high school.

In 1997, a little over ten years later, that series ended and soon after, the company Her Interactive released a video game called *Secrets Can Kill* based on that first book of the Nancy Drew Files. They went on to release many more games filled with clues to find and puzzles to solve.

The publisher also wanted to create a Nancy for younger readers, ages five to eight. In 1994, the Nancy Drew Notebooks featured third-grade Nancy. In the first book, *The Slumber Party Secret*, Nancy goes to her first slumber party and gets

to solve her first-ever case! She uncovers the secret behind stolen invitations, suspicious notes, and a missing icing rose from the cake. This series was released again in 2006 as Nancy Drew and the Clue Crew.

Nancy Drew reached new readers of all ages. But the case was not yet closed on the fearless detective.

CHAPTER 9
A Modern Girl

Nancy Drew: Girl Detective, a series for Nancy's original audience of eight-to-twelve-year-olds, began in 2004. In the first book, *Without a Trace*, Nancy starts by talking straight to the reader. "My name is Nancy Drew," she says. "My friends tell me I'm always looking for trouble, but that's not really true. It just seems to have a way of finding me." This twenty-first-century Nancy reflected the ideas of her time. She cares about the environment by driving a hybrid car. She supports her community by volunteering to build apartments and help out at charity bike races. She uses her computer, cell phone, and GPS. She takes flying lessons, studies monkeys in Costa Rica, visits a spa, and digs for dinosaur bones.

Her cases involve virtual reality games, beauty pageants, reality-show stars, and even UFOs.

Also in the early 2000s, pictures and stories

came together in graphic novel versions of Nancy Drew. The publisher Papercutz launched *Nancy Drew, Girl Detective: The Demon of River Heights* in 2005. The comic artists created very modern versions of Nancy and her pals George, Bess, and Ned.

The next decade had another new Nancy Drew series as well. In 2013, the Nancy Drew Diaries began with Nancy, Bess, and George boarding a cruise ship for a mystery at sea! This series revisited some classic themes from early books—like lakeside camping adventures and haunted houses. It also included more recent details, like podcasts and social media. In 2019, another comic version of Nancy declares, "Let no one say the life of Nancy Drew is boring." That's for sure!

Books were never enough for the Nancy Drew character. Once again, she left River Heights for Hollywood to star in the movies. In 2007's *Nancy Drew*, actress Emma Roberts plays the title character. The story follows Nancy's move with her father to Los Angeles, where she has to solve a celebrity murder mystery. In 2019, Nancy stepped onto screens again with *Nancy Drew and the Hidden Staircase*, starring Sophia Lillis. This time, she explores the source of the secret behind the flickering lights, spooky sounds, and strange figures in a haunted house. No car for Nancy in this version. She rides a skateboard!

Kennedy McMann

The year 2020 would be a big one for Nancy. She had reached her ninetieth anniversary! In the run-up to this major event, the CW television network released the show *Nancy Drew* in 2019, with a totally modern Nancy played by Kennedy McMann.

This latest version of Nancy works at the Bayside Claw restaurant in Horseshoe Bay, Maine. When a wealthy woman mysteriously dies, Nancy and her friends Bess, George, and Ned become murder suspects. To make matters worse, Horseshoe Bay is also haunted by the ghost of a beauty queen. This modern Nancy is not perfect, like the Nancy of the old days. But she is smart, brave, and works hard to fight for what's right. Fans had fun finding references to the old Nancy books in the CW series. Nancy drives a blue car. The town has a Keene High School and Lilac Inn. And there is a family named Tandy, after the illustrator Russell H. Tandy.

Pamela Sue Martin, who appeared in the TV show in the 1970s, plays a psychic who can talk to ghosts in one of the episodes.

Nancy's fans come in all ages because people have been reading stories and watching shows about Nancy for almost a century! Lots of famous women, including television host Oprah

Winfrey, former secretary of state Hillary Clinton, author Judy Blume, Supreme Court justice Sonia Sotomayor, and former first lady Laura Bush have said that Nancy inspired them. Collectors buy and trade Nancy souvenirs. Many fans visit flea markets and tag sales to find copies of the older books.

Since Nancy first appeared in 1930, more than six hundred Nancy Drew books have been written under the pen name Carolyn Keene. Through the years, Nancy has proved she can do it all. Her story is filled with thrills and danger, fun and friendships, and mysterious adventures. She never seems to need rescuing—she's the one who comes to the rescue! Nancy is a hero, not only in her own stories but for her countless readers. She has inspired kids to be adventurous, curious problem-solvers who get the job done.

Bibliography

*Books for young readers

Billman, Carol. *The Secret of the Stratemeyer Syndicate: Nancy Drew, the Hardy Boys, and the Million Dollar Fiction Factory*. New York: The Ungar Publishing Company, 1986.

*Keene, Carolyn. *The Secret of the Old Clock*. 1930. Facsimile of the first edition. Bedford, MA: Applewood Books, 1991.

Kismaric, Carole, and Marvin Heiferman. *The Mysterious Case of Nancy Drew and the Hardy Boys*. New York: Simon & Schuster, 1998.

Lapin, Geoffrey S. "The Ghost of Nancy Drew." *Books at Iowa* 50 (1), April 1989. https://doi.org/10.17077/0006-7474.1164.

O'Rourke, Meghan. "Nancy Drew's Father: The Fiction Factory of Edward Stratemeyer." *New Yorker*, November 8, 2004.

Plunkett-Powell, Karen. *The Nancy Drew Scrapbook: 60 Years of America's Favorite Teenage Sleuth*. New York: St. Martin's Press, 1993.

Politowicz, Tracy Ann. "The mystery of Nancy Drew: 90 years later, the iconic sleuth is still on the case." *The Star-Ledger*, May 6, 2020. https://www.nj.com/entertainment/2020/04/the-mystery-of-nancy-drew-90-years-later-the-iconic-sleuth-is-still-on-the-case.html.

Rehak, Melanie. *Girl Sleuth: Nancy Drew and the Women Who Created Her*. Orlando, FL: Harcourt, Inc., 2005.

*Rubini, Julie K. *Missing Millie Benson: The Secret Case of the Nancy Drew Ghostwriter and Journalist*. Athens, OH: Ohio University Press, 2015.

Website

The Nancy Drew Sleuth Unofficial Website: www.nancydrewsleuth.com

Timeline of Nancy Drew

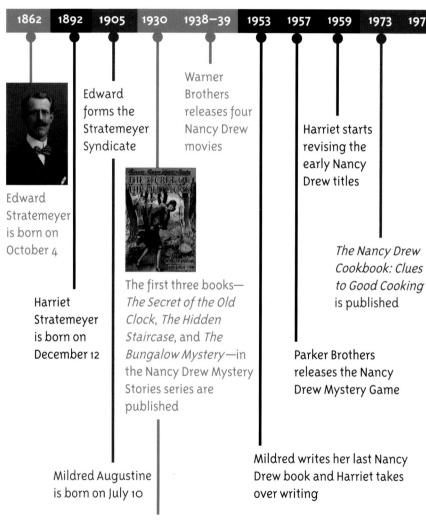

1862 · **1892** · **1905** · **1930** · **1938–39** · **1953** · **1957** · **1959** · **1973** · **1977–**

Edward forms the Stratemeyer Syndicate

Warner Brothers releases four Nancy Drew movies

Harriet starts revising the early Nancy Drew titles

Edward Stratemeyer is born on October 4

Harriet Stratemeyer is born on December 12

The first three books—*The Secret of the Old Clock*, *The Hidden Staircase*, and *The Bungalow Mystery*—in the Nancy Drew Mystery Stories series are published

The Nancy Drew Cookbook: Clues to Good Cooking is published

Parker Brothers releases the Nancy Drew Mystery Game

Mildred Augustine is born on July 10

Mildred writes her last Nancy Drew book and Harriet takes over writing

Edward dies

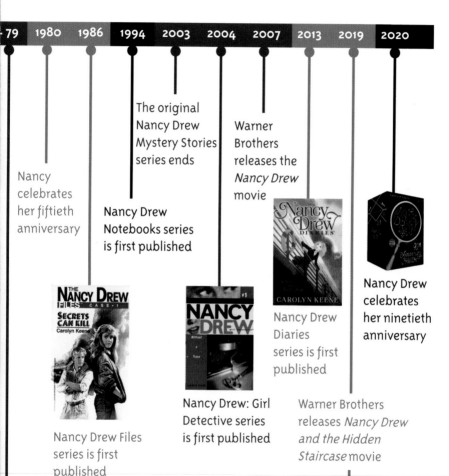

| -79 | 1980 | 1986 | 1994 | 2003 | 2004 | 2007 | 2013 | 2019 | 2020 |

The original Nancy Drew Mystery Stories series ends

Warner Brothers releases the *Nancy Drew* movie

Nancy celebrates her fiftieth anniversary

Nancy Drew Notebooks series is first published

Nancy Drew Diaries series is first published

Nancy Drew celebrates her ninetieth anniversary

Nancy Drew Files series is first published

Nancy Drew: Girl Detective series is first published

Warner Brothers releases *Nancy Drew and the Hidden Staircase* movie

ABC airs the family television series *The Hardy Boys/Nancy Drew Mysteries*

The CW airs the *Nancy Drew* television series

Photo credit: (portrait of Edward Stratemeyer) public domain, via New York Public Library, Manuscripts and Archives Division